100

IQ

Questions

Zoe Hampton

Other IQ books by the author
https://prfc.nl/go/amznbooks

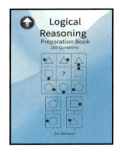
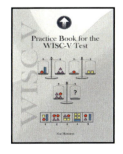
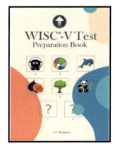

Our Mobile Applications for IQ Training

https://prfc.nl/go/allapps

Follow us on social media

Web site: https://prfc.nl/go/pc

Facebook: https://prfc.nl/go/fbpc

Instagram: https://prfc.nl/go/inpc

LinkedIn: https://prfc.nl/go/lipc

YouTube: https://prfc.nl/go/ytpc

Table of Contents

Introduction

This book contains 100 IQ questions - 10 types of IQ tests with 10 questions each. The questions are designed to assess your mental abilities and skills. Working through the questions will help you improve your concentration and develop the ability to interpret patterns, number sequences or the relationships between shapes.

Training your logic skills with this book will improve your IQ and build a strong foundation for academic and personal success. If you are faced with a IQ test during an assessment and have practiced with this book, you will perform much better than before.

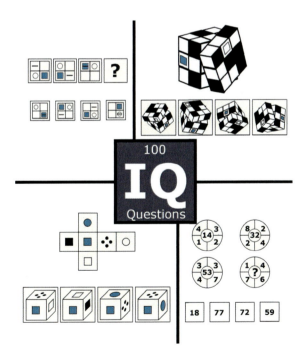

The IQ questions in this book are designed to assess a variety of mental abilities and skills and therefore cover a wide range of different types of intelligence. The questions are grouped by types and 10 questions of each type is included. The list of question types which can be found below:

- Spatial Reasoning Test
- Diagrammatic Reasoning Test
- Deductive Reasoning Test With Figures
- Inductive Reasoning Figure Series Test
- Math Riddles Test
- Abstract Reasoning Test
- Logical Reasoning Test
- Inductive Reasoning Test
- Number Series Test
- Verbal Reasoning Test With Analogies

Disclaimer: This test is intended for informational and entertainment purposes only.

<u>Spatial Reasoning Test</u>

Spatial reasoning is a category of logical thinking that refers to the ability to think about objects in three dimensions and to draw conclusions about those objects from limited information. Someone with good spatial skills is also good at thinking about how an object will look when it is rotated. These skills are valuable in many real-world situations and can be improved with practice.

<u>Instructions:</u>
You are presented with a 2D net of (usually) a cube or cuboid, and you must identify which of the answer choices cannot be generated by this 2D net. The challenge is that each side of the shape has a particular pattern or colour. This requires you to mentally figure out what each side will look like when folded and rotated - pay attention to how the patterns can change when rotated and turned in 3D.

Spatial Reasoning Test

Question 1: Which cube cannot be made based on the unfolded cube?

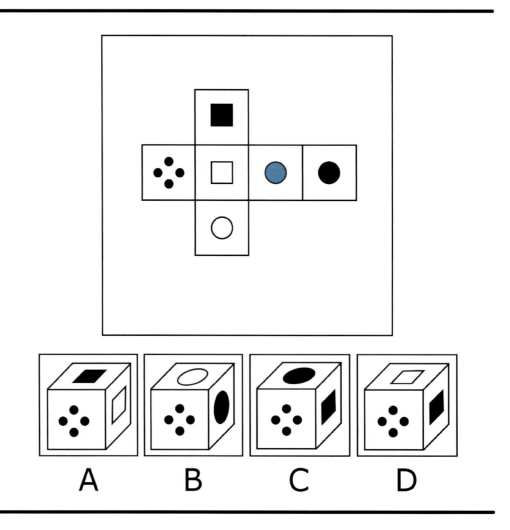

Spatial Reasoning Test

Question 2: Which cube cannot be made based on the unfolded cube?

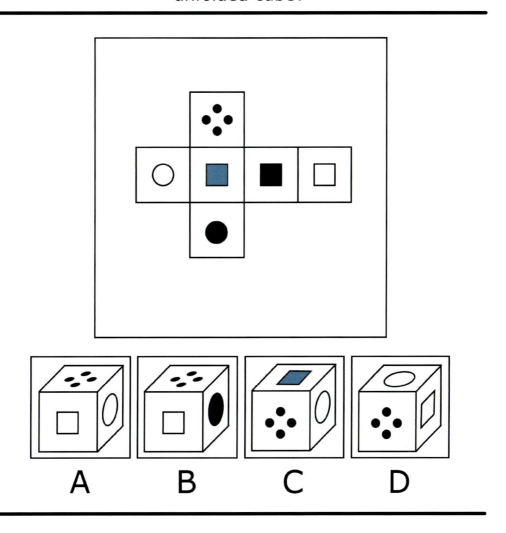

Spatial Reasoning Test

Question 3: Which cube cannot be made based on the unfolded cube?

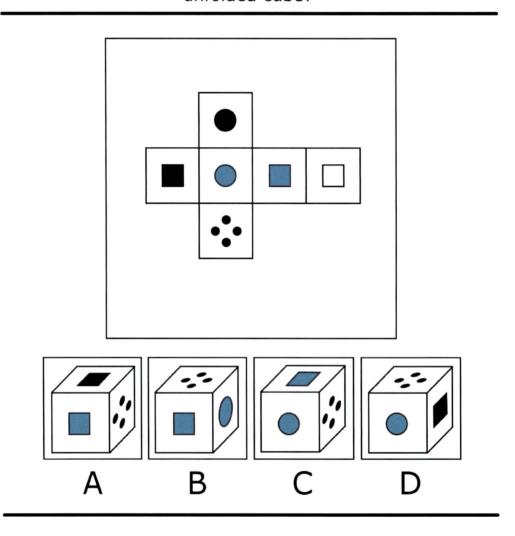

Spatial Reasoning Test

Question 4: Which cube cannot be made based on the unfolded cube?

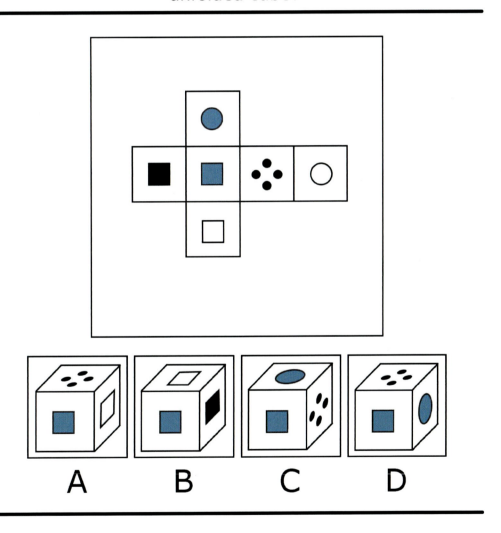

Spatial Reasoning Test

Question 5: Which cube cannot be made based on the unfolded cube?

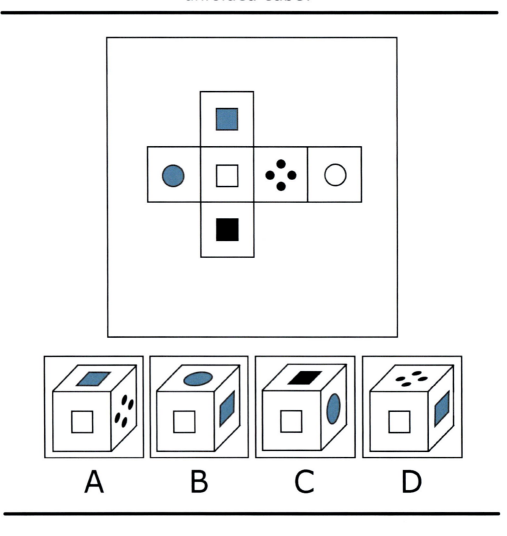

A   B   C   D

Spatial Reasoning Test

Question 6: Which figure is a rotation of the given object?

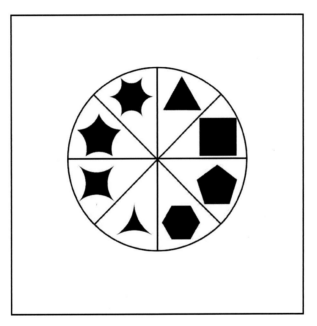

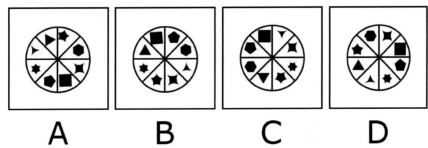

A B C D

Spatial Reasoning Test

Question 7: Which figure is a rotation of the given object?

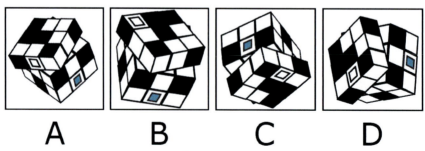

A   B   C   D

Spatial Reasoning Test

Question 8: Which figure is a rotation of the given object?

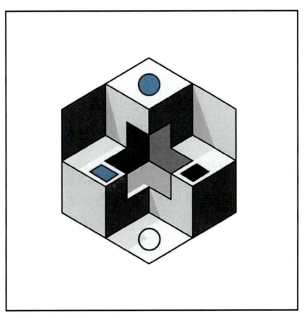

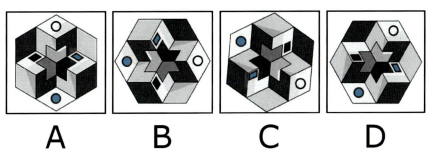

A   B   C   D

Spatial Reasoning Test

Question 9: Which figure fits the given object, in order to make a square with 100 cubes?

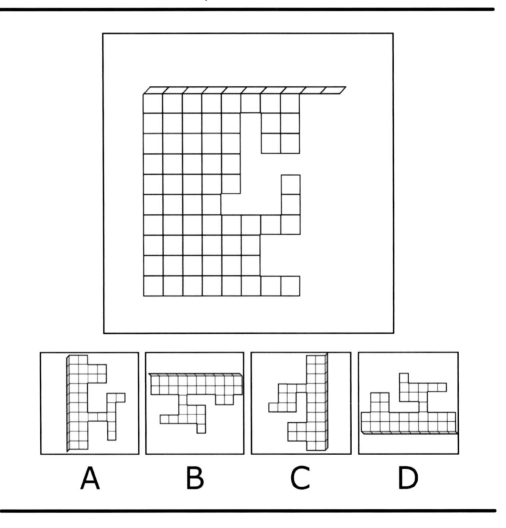

A   B   C   D

Spatial Reasoning Test

Question 10: Which figure is a rotation of the given object?

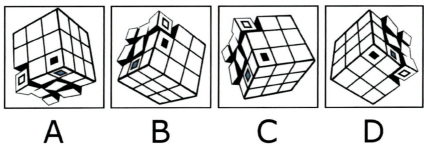

A   B   C   D

Diagrammatic Reasoning Test

The construct of diagrammatic reasoning is about understanding concepts and information visualized using diagrams and figures. In a diagram test, you are presented with a picture of numbers, symbols, and arrows. Each number or symbol represents an operation. You can think of these operations as mathematical functions. However, instead of multiplying or dividing, you will rearrange shapes, rotate, and swap symbols.

Instructions:
The first eight questions show a diagram of four operators with an explanation of their behavior and an incomplete operator. Find out which operator(s) or figure replaces the question mark. The last two questions contain two groups of figures and a separate figure. Find out to which of the two groups the figure logically belongs.

Diagrammatic Reasoning Test

Question 1: Which operator replaces the question mark?

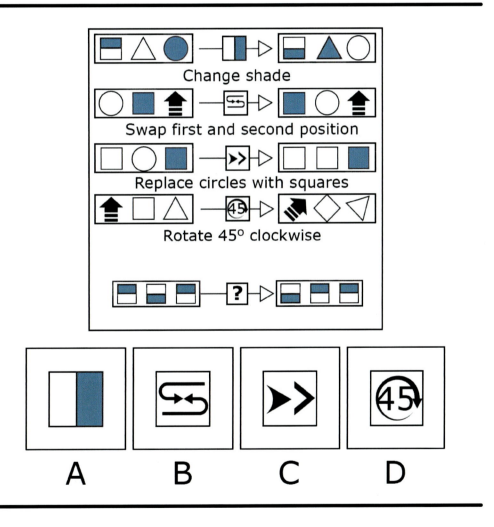

Diagrammatic Reasoning Test

Question 2: Which operator replaces the question mark?

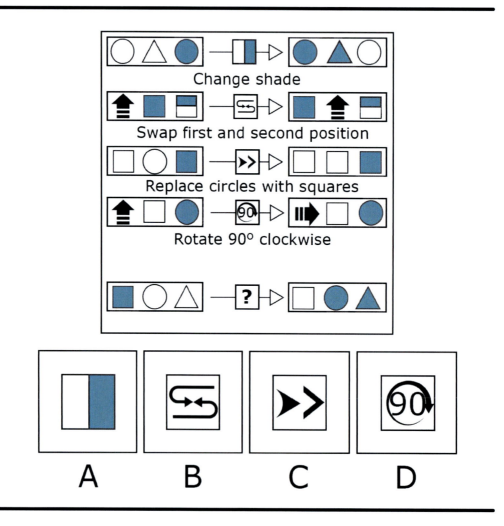

Diagrammatic Reasoning Test

Question 3: Which operator replaces the question mark?

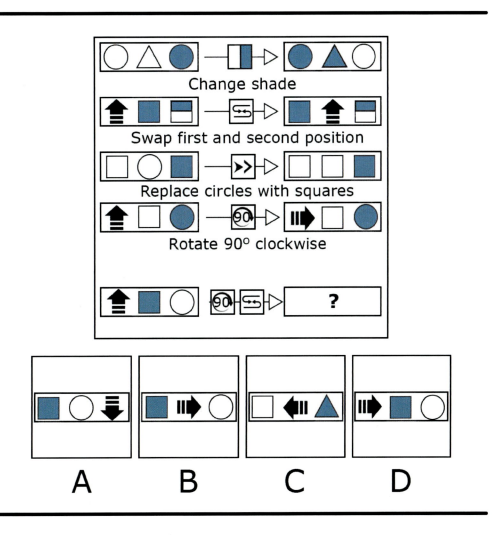

Diagrammatic Reasoning Test

Question 4: Which operator replaces the question mark?

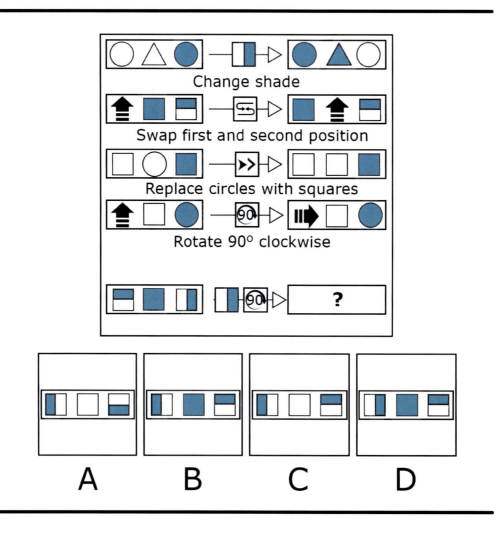

Diagrammatic Reasoning Test

Question 5: Which operator replaces the question mark?

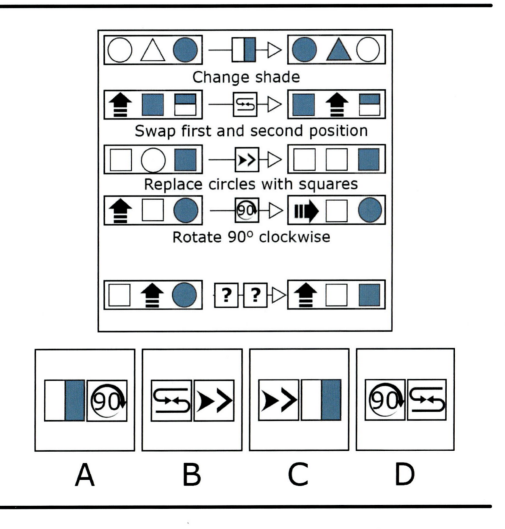

A   B   C   D

Diagrammatic Reasoning Test

Question 6: Which operator replaces the question mark?

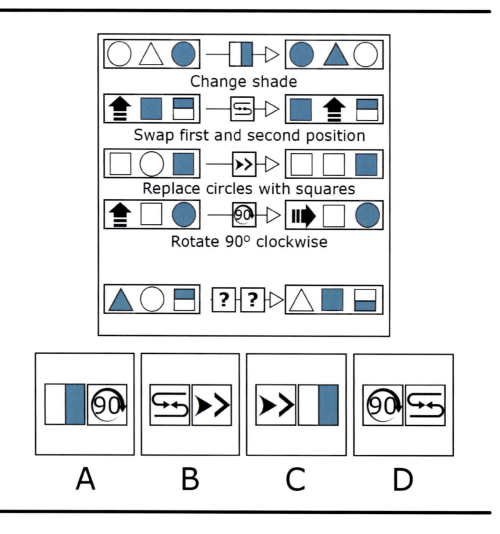

Diagrammatic Reasoning Test

Question 7: Which operator replaces the question mark?

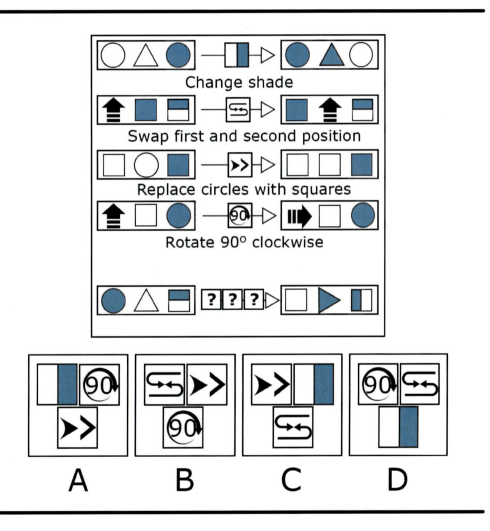

 is described above.

A   B   C   D

Diagrammatic Reasoning Test

Question 8: Which operator replaces the question mark?

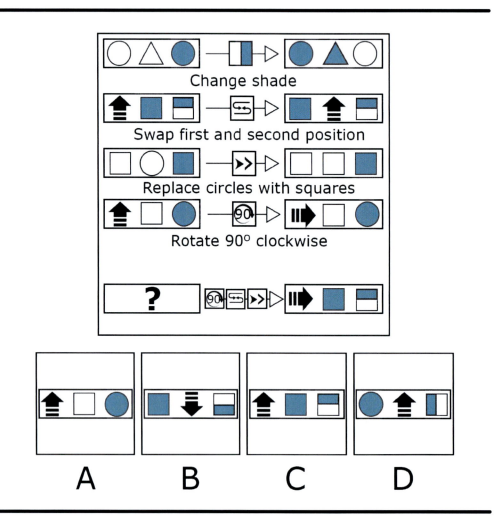

A   B   C   D

Diagrammatic Reasoning Test

Question 9: To which group does the figure belong?

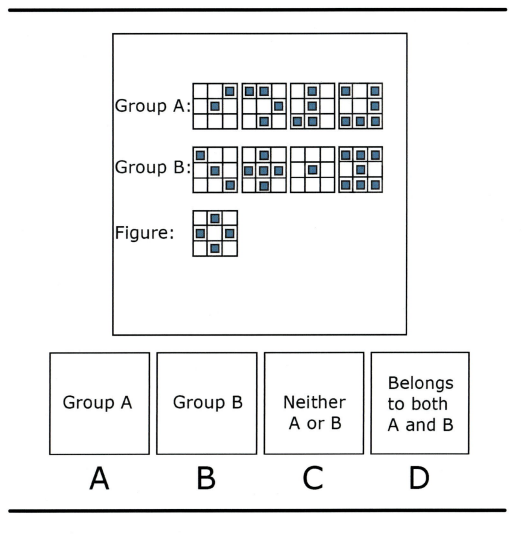

Group A	Group B	Neither A or B	Belongs to both A and B
A	B	C	D

Diagrammatic Reasoning Test

Question 10: To which group does the figure belong?

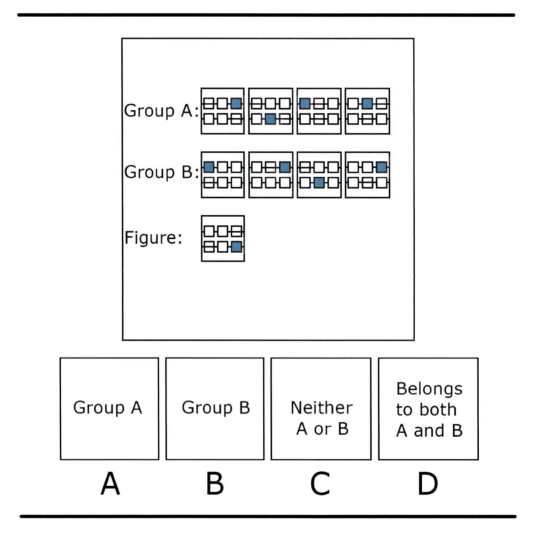

Group A	Group B	Neither A or B	Belongs to both A and B
A	B	C	D

Deductive Reasoning Test With Figures

Deductive reasoning is sometimes called top-down reasoning, which means drawing a conclusion about a particular case from a general rule. The word deduce, by the way, comes from the Latin word deducere, which means "to deduce."

In deductive reasoning exercises, you are expected to take a law given in a premise and show that it applies in different cases. Deductive reasoning uses certain facts and established patterns; therefore, it allows us to formulate definite conclusions, as you would in science or mathematics, where a particular solution is guaranteed.

Deductive reasoning is actually less about solving problems and more about interpreting and applying rules. Since you have to base every step of your reasoning on the premises, there isn't much room for creativity and exploration.

Instructions:
-      A row or column never contains the same figure twice.
-      Every row and column contain the same figures.

Deductive Reasoning Test With Figures

Question 1: Which figure replaces the question mark?

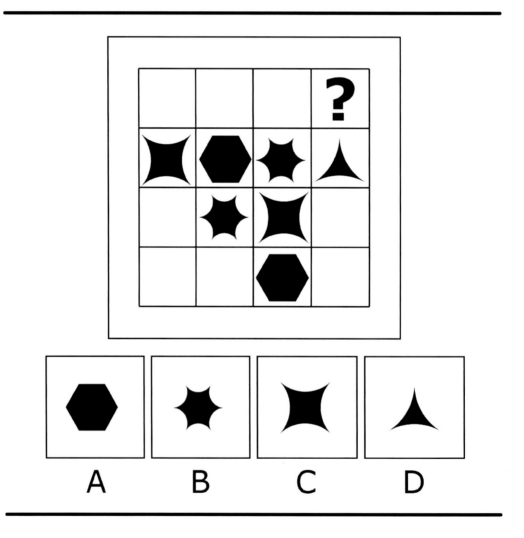

Deductive Reasoning Test With Figures

Question 2: Which figure replaces the question mark?

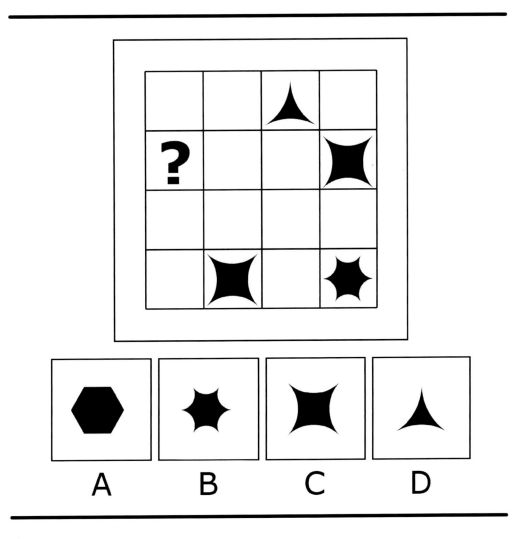

Deductive Reasoning Test With Figures

Question 3: Which figure replaces the question mark?

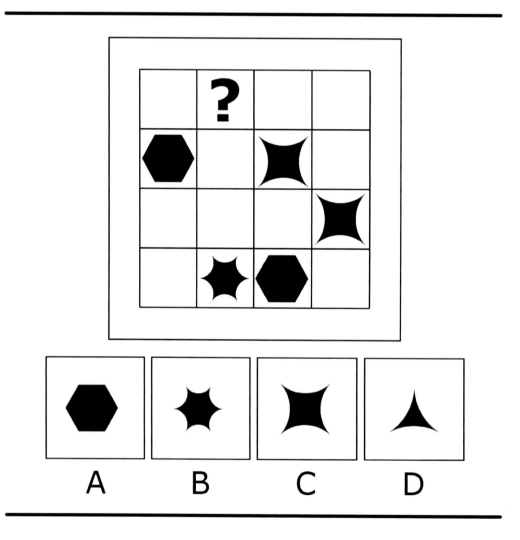

Deductive Reasoning Test With Figures

Question 4: Which figure replaces the question mark?

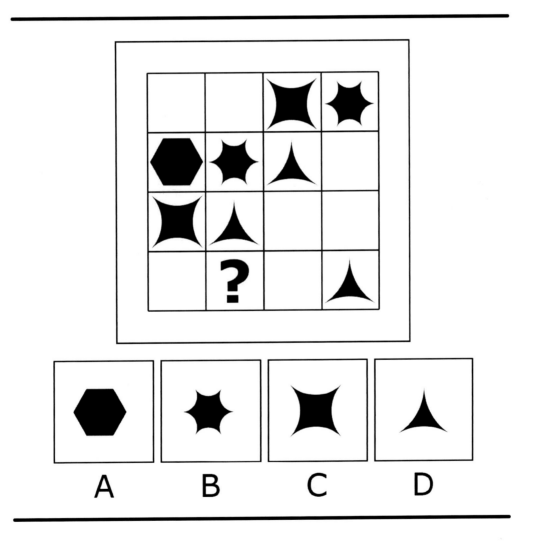

Deductive Reasoning Test With Figures

Question 5: Which figure replaces the question mark?

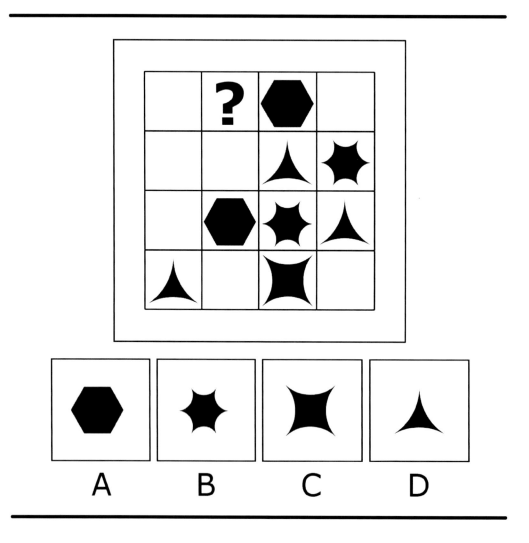

Deductive Reasoning Test With Figures

Question 6: Which figure replaces the question mark?

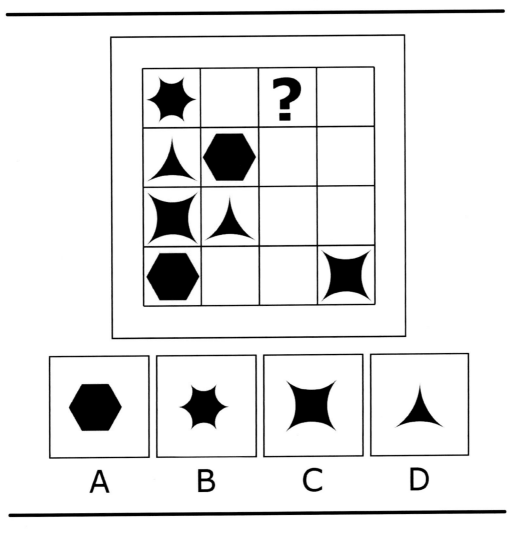

Deductive Reasoning Test With Figures

Question 7: Which figure replaces the question mark?

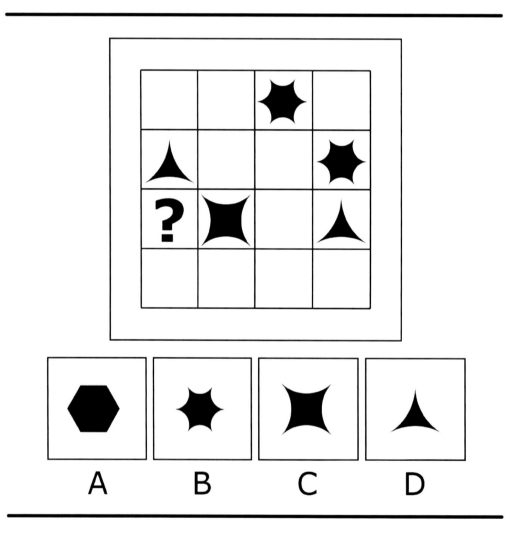

Deductive Reasoning Test With Figures

Question 8: Which figure replaces the question mark?

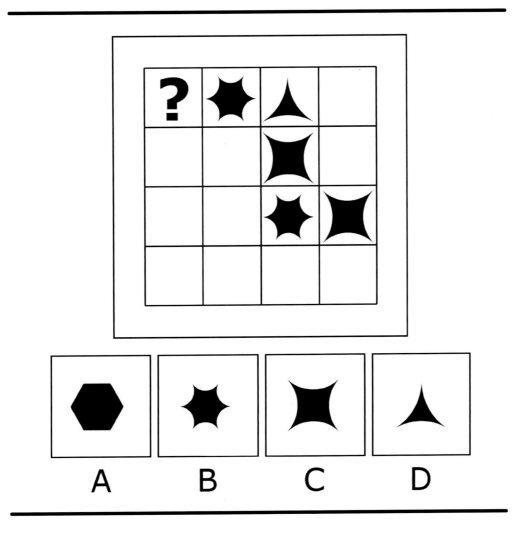

Deductive Reasoning Test With Figures

Question 9: Which figure replaces the question mark?

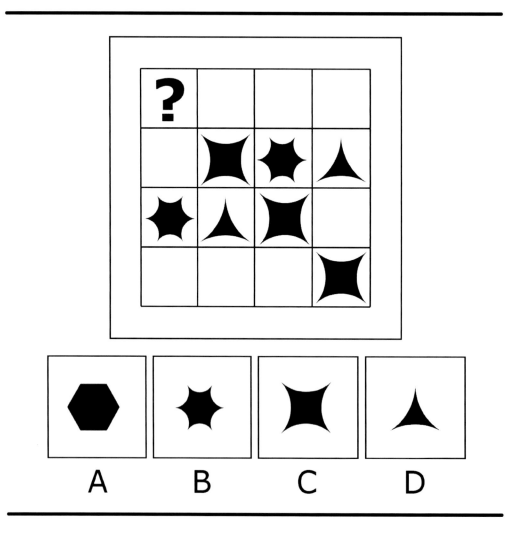

Deductive Reasoning Test With Figures

Question 10: Which figure replaces the question mark?

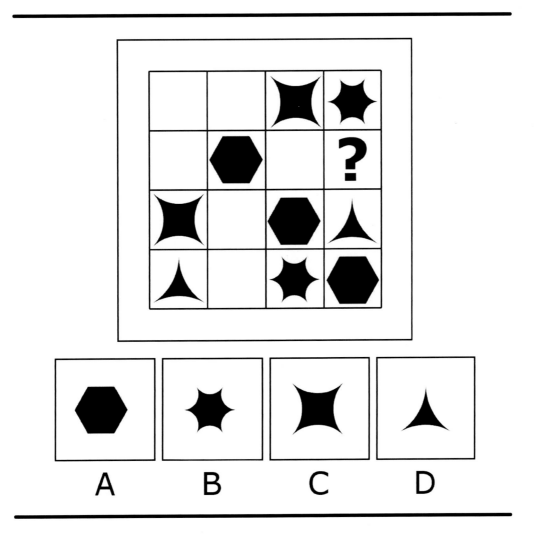

Inductive Reasoning Figure Series Test

Inductive reasoning is a basic form of logical processing. Induction is logic from the bottom up. Instead of starting with a proven theory, you take a set of observations and develop an argument to explain them. Inductive reasoning allows us to make generalisations that allow us to better understand our surroundings.

Instructions:
In each of the following tests of inductive reasoning, there are a series of graphs that follow a pattern. The goal is to determine which of the possible four options would logically follow in order. Only one of the given options is correct.

Inductive Reasoning Figure Series Test

Question 1: Which pattern best completes the sequence or matrix?

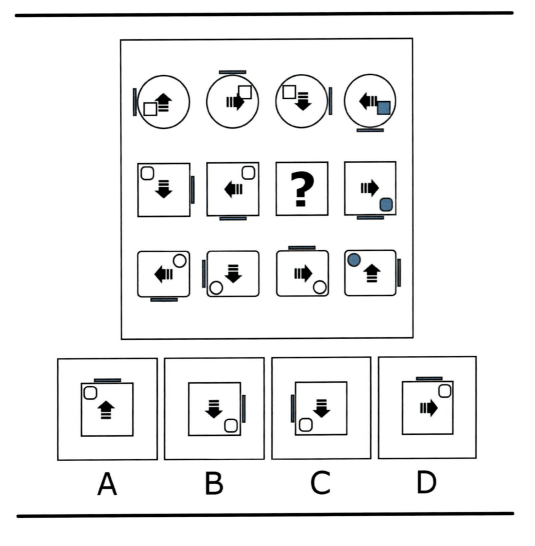

Inductive Reasoning Figure Series Test

Question 2: Which pattern best completes the sequence or matrix?

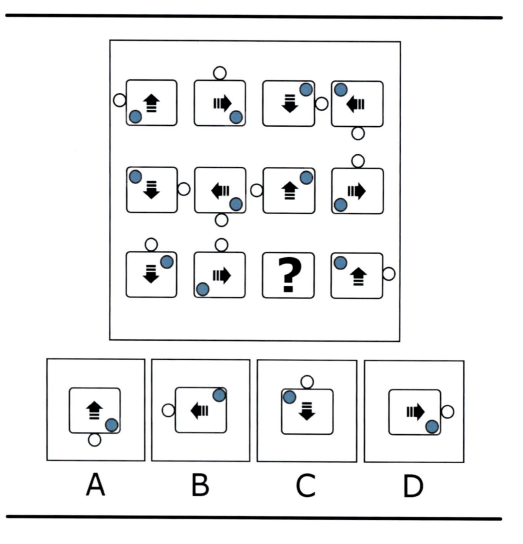

Inductive Reasoning Figure Series Test

Question 3: Which pattern best completes the sequence or matrix?

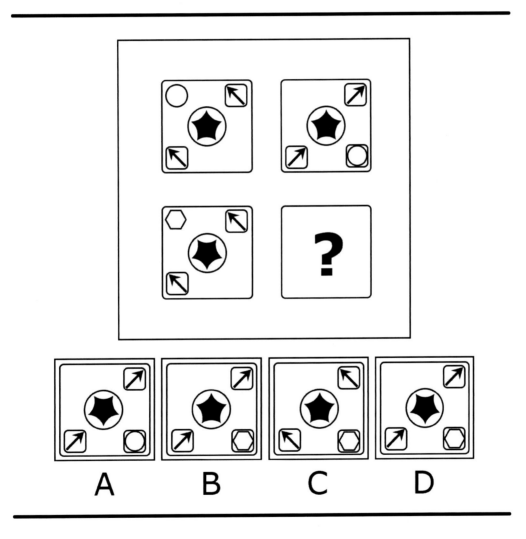

Inductive Reasoning Figure Series Test

Question 4: Which pattern best completes the sequence or matrix?

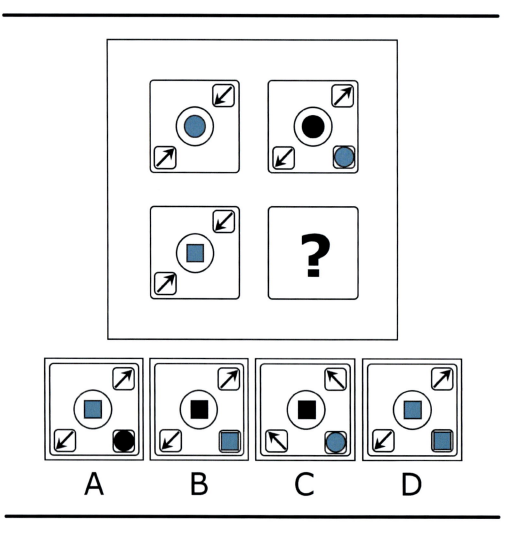

Inductive Reasoning Figure Series Test

Question 5: Which pattern best completes the sequence or matrix?

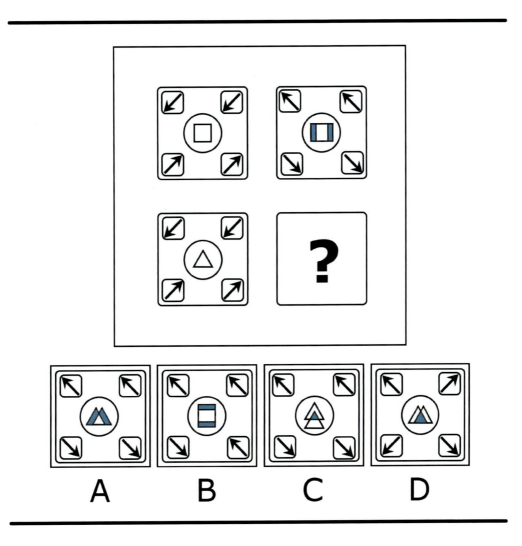

Inductive Reasoning Figure Series Test

Question 6: Which pattern best completes the sequence or matrix?

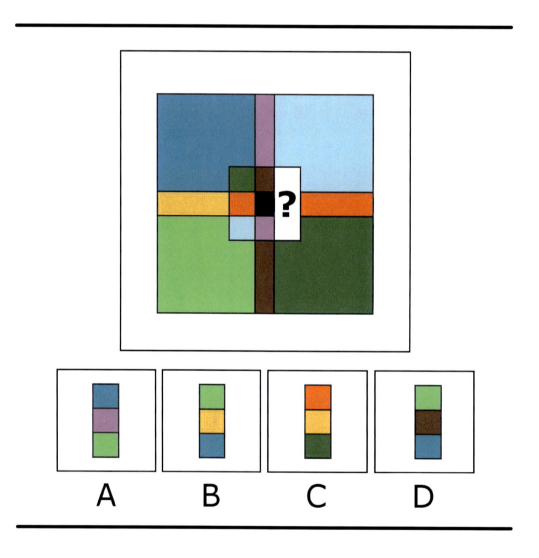

A   B   C   D

Inductive Reasoning Figure Series Test

Question 7: Which pattern best completes the sequence or matrix?

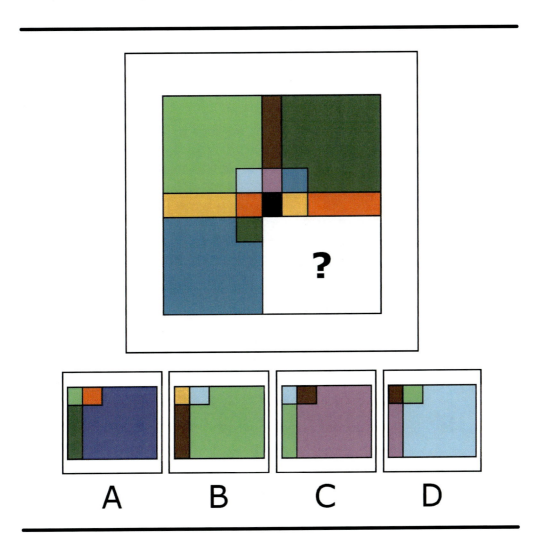

Inductive Reasoning Figure Series Test

Question 8: Which pattern best completes the sequence or matrix?

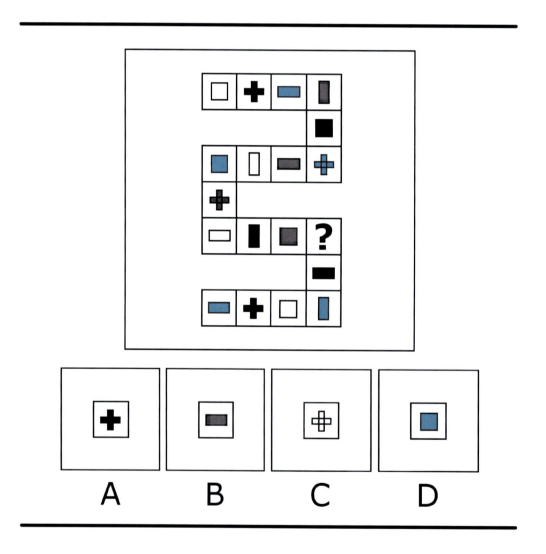

Inductive Reasoning Figure Series Test

Question 9: Which pattern best completes the sequence or matrix?

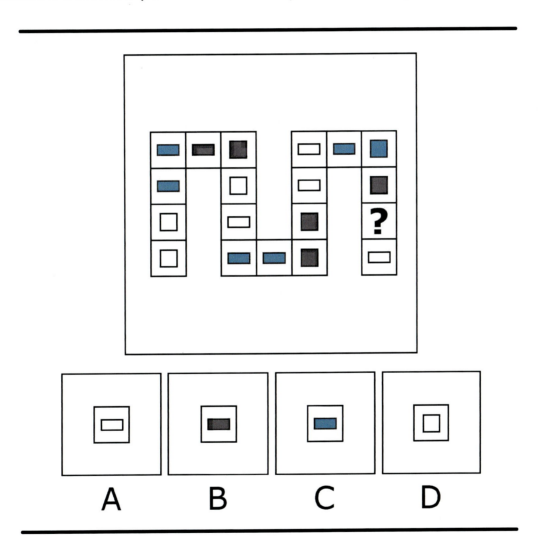

Inductive Reasoning Figure Series Test

Question 10: Which pattern best completes the sequence or matrix?

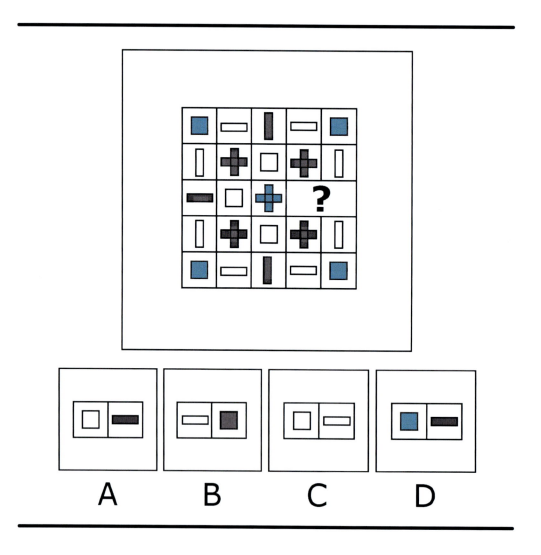

A   B   C   D

Math Riddles Test

Math riddles and number puzzles that challenge your lateral thinking. Math Riddles tests your IQ with math puzzles. You'll exercise both parts of your brain by exploring the relationships between numbers in geometric figures.

Instructions:
You will solve the relationship between numbers in the geometrical figures, and complete the missing numbers at the end.

Math Riddles Test

Question 1: What number should replace the question mark?

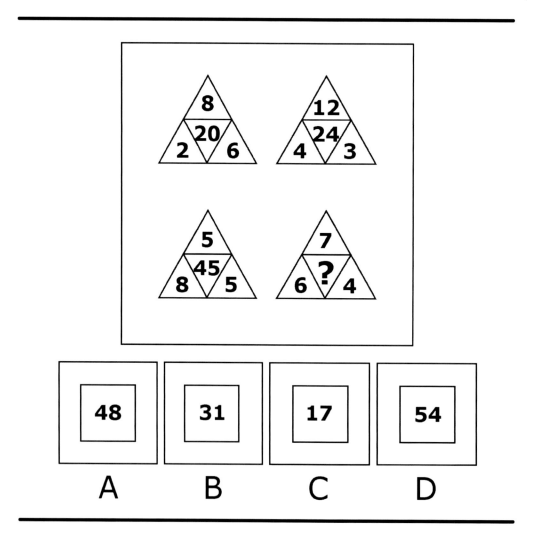

Math Riddles Test

Question 2: What number should replace the question mark?

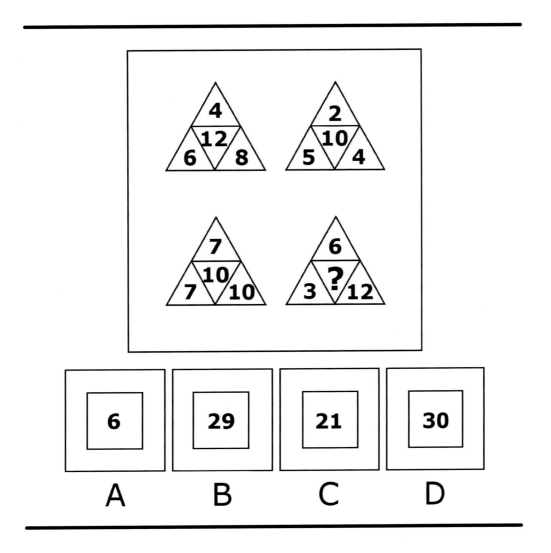

Math Riddles Test

Question 3: What number should replace the question mark?

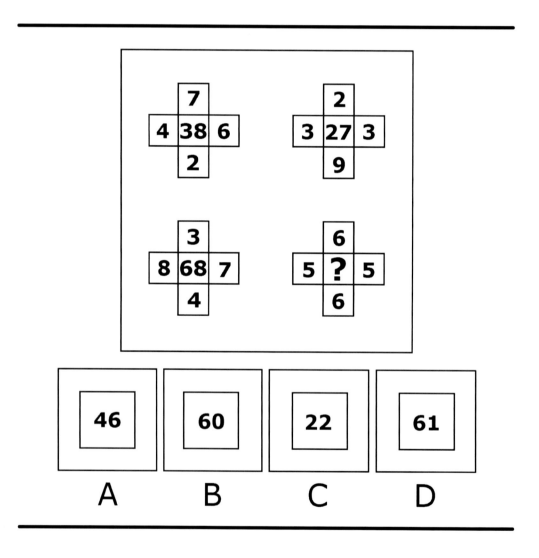

Math Riddles Test

Question 4: What number should replace the question mark?

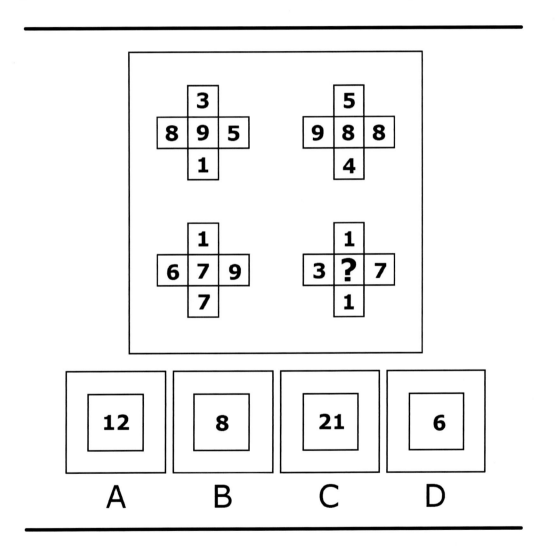

Math Riddles Test

Question 5: What number should replace the question mark?

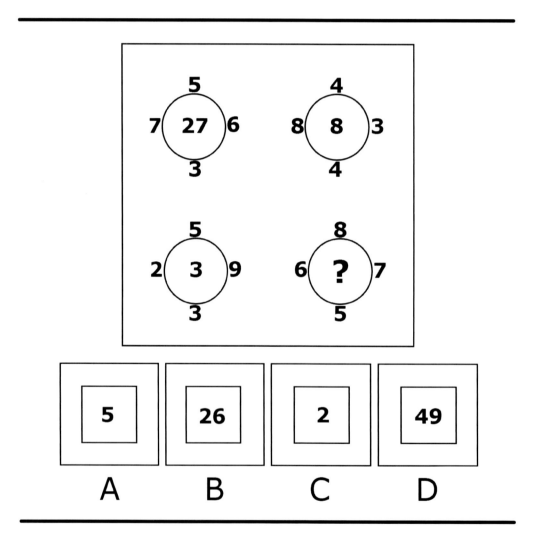

A   B   C   D

Math Riddles Test

Question 6: What number should replace the question mark?

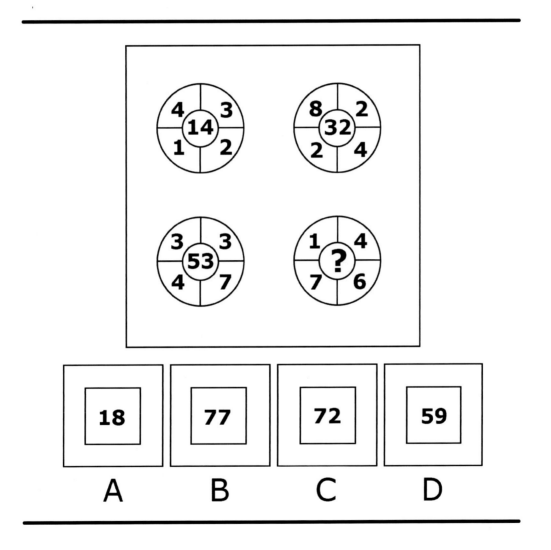

18	77	72	59
A	B	C	D

Math Riddles Test

Question 7:To which figure does the square belong?

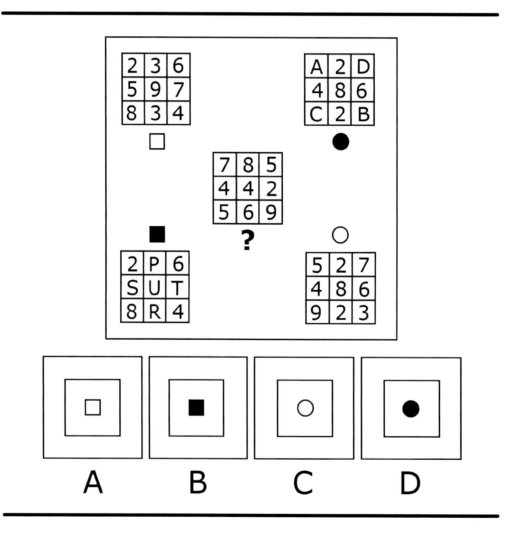

Math Riddles Test

Question 8: What number should replace the question mark?

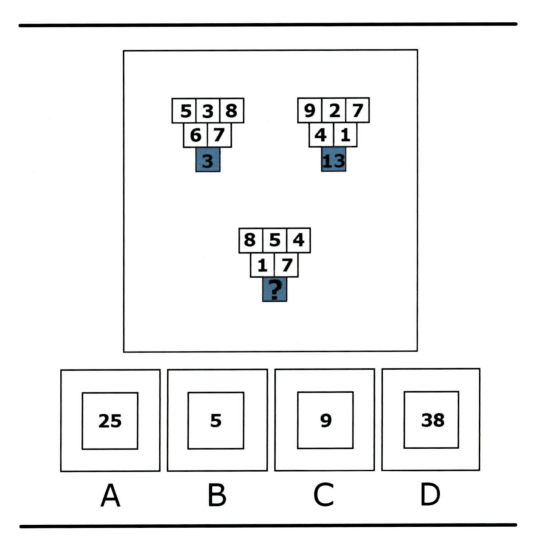

A. 25 B. 5 C. 9 D. 38

Math Riddles Test

Question 9: What number should replace the question mark?

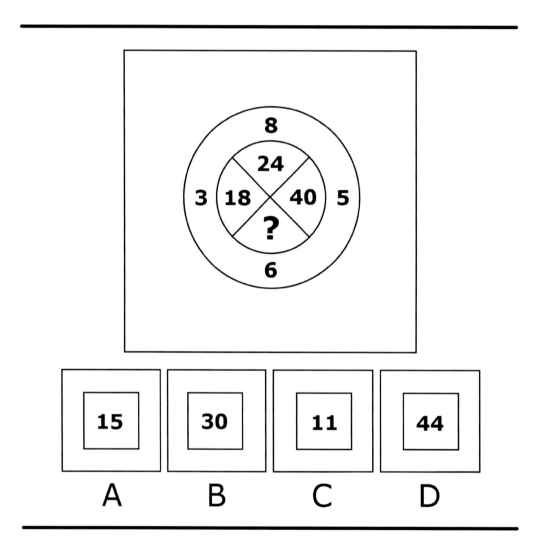

Math Riddles Test

Question 10: What number should replace the question mark?

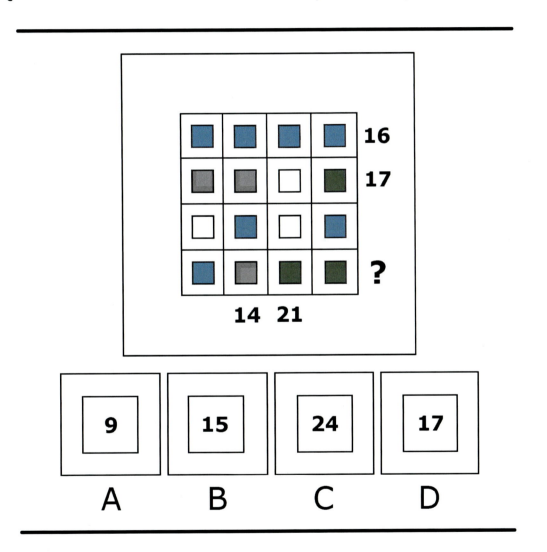

A	B	C	D
9	15	24	17

Abstract Reasoning Test

A test of abstract reasoning assesses your inductive logic. That is, your ability to recognize patterns, analyse data, and make connexions. Abstract reasoning generally does not require verbal or numerical reasoning.

Instructions:

In an abstract reasoning test, you are shown a series of shapes arranged in either a sequence or a matrix and asked to identify the missing piece in the puzzle.

Abstract Reasoning Test

Question 1: Which figure completes the series?

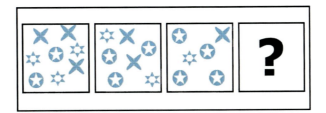

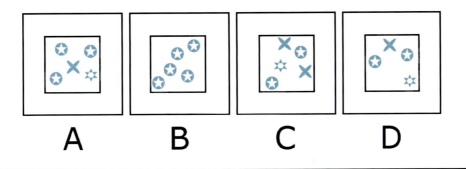

A   B   C   D

Abstract Reasoning Test

Question 2: Which figure completes the series?

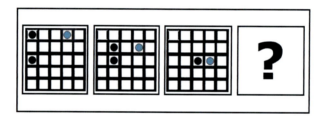

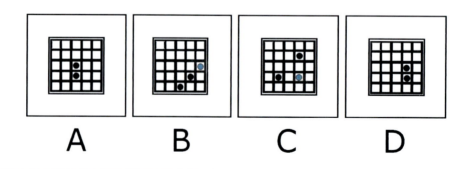

| A | B | C | D |

Abstract Reasoning Test

Question 3: Which figure completes the series?

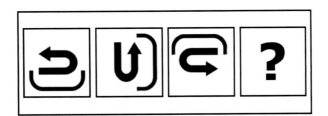

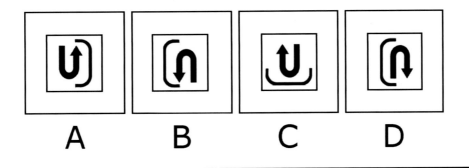

Abstract Reasoning Test

Question 4: Which figure completes the series?

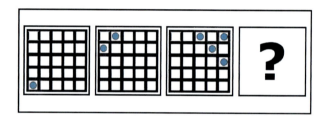

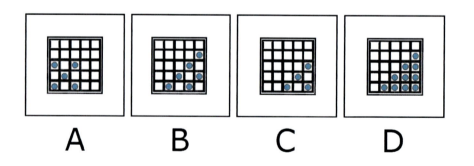

A   B   C   D

Abstract Reasoning Test

Question 5: Which figure completes the series?

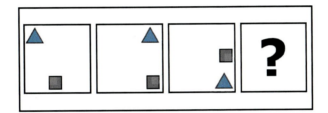

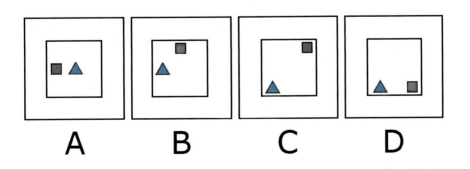

A   B   C   D

Abstract Reasoning Test

Question 6: Which figure completes the series?

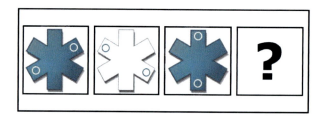

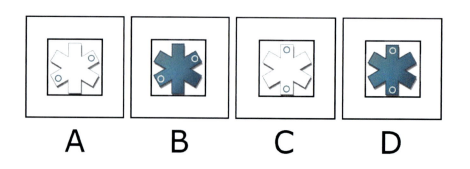

A   B   C   D

Abstract Reasoning Test

Question 7: Which figure completes the series?

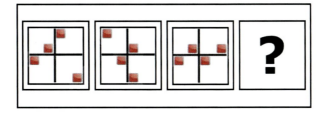

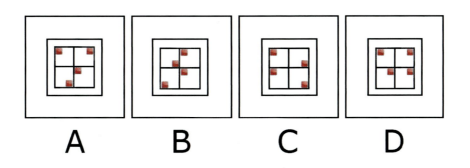

Abstract Reasoning Test

Question 8: Which figure completes the series?

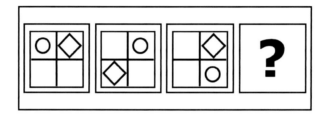

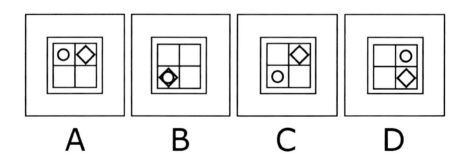

A B C D

Abstract Reasoning Test

Question 9: Which figure completes the series?

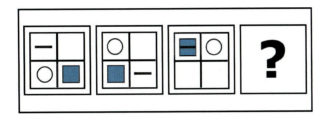

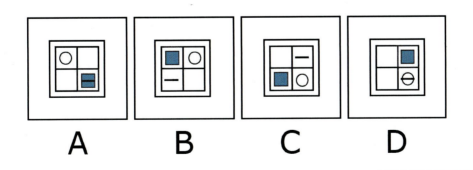

A   B   C   D

Abstract Reasoning Test

Question 10: Which figure completes the series?

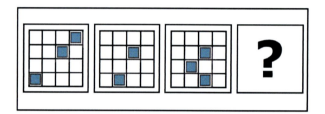

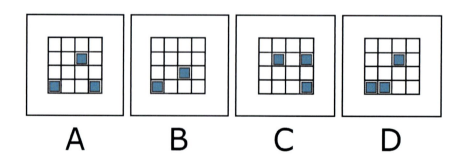

A   B   C   D

Logical Reasoning Test

A logical reasoning test determines your ability to interpret information and then apply a systematic process to solve problems and draw relevant conclusions. Logical reasoning tests assess your abilities, such as how you can interpret patterns or relationships between shapes.

Instructions:
The questions require you to look at the patterns in the squares and understand their relationship to each other in order to identify the missing square.

Logical Reasoning Test

Question 1: Which of the following images completes the missing part?

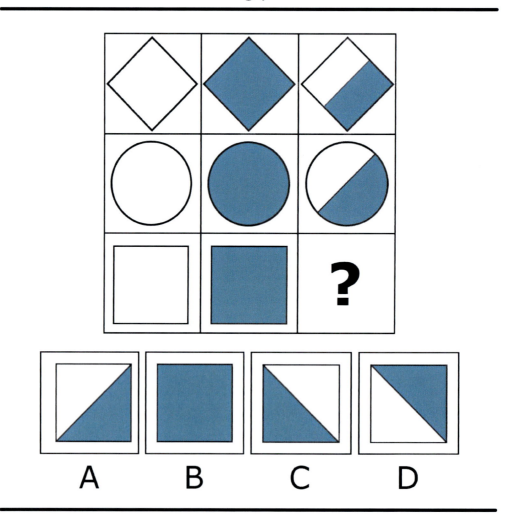

Logical Reasoning Test

Question 2: Which of the following images completes the missing part?

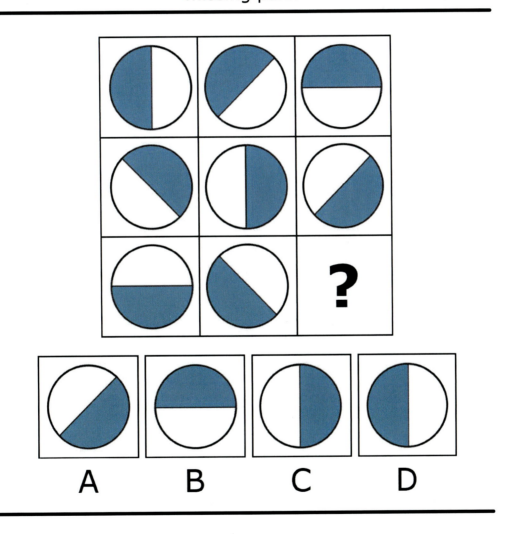

Logical Reasoning Test

Question 3: Which of the following images completes the missing part?

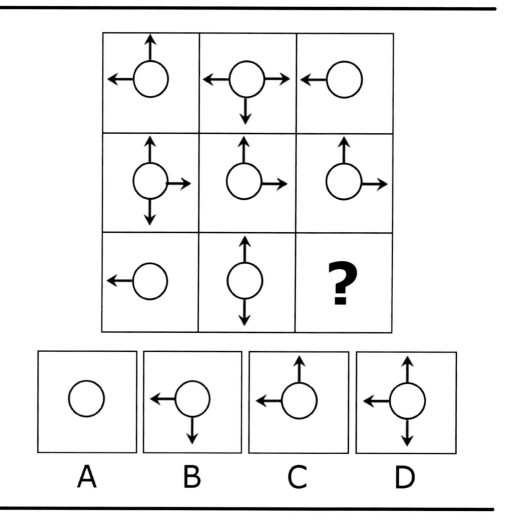

Logical Reasoning Test

Question 4: Which of the following images completes the missing part?

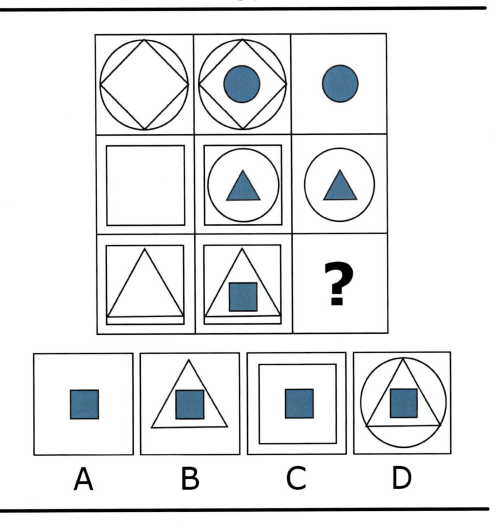

Logical Reasoning Test

Question 5: Which of the following images completes the missing part?

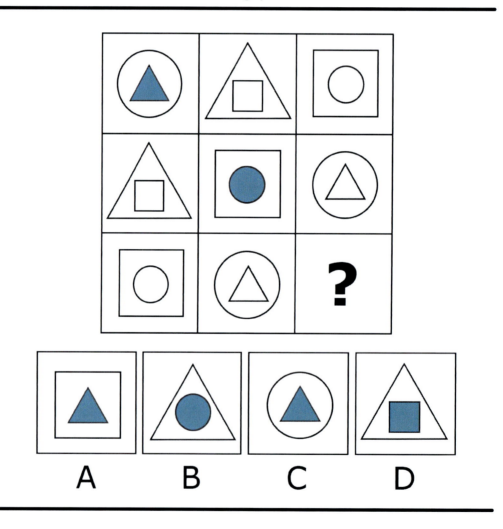

Logical Reasoning Test

Question 6: Which of the following images completes the missing part?

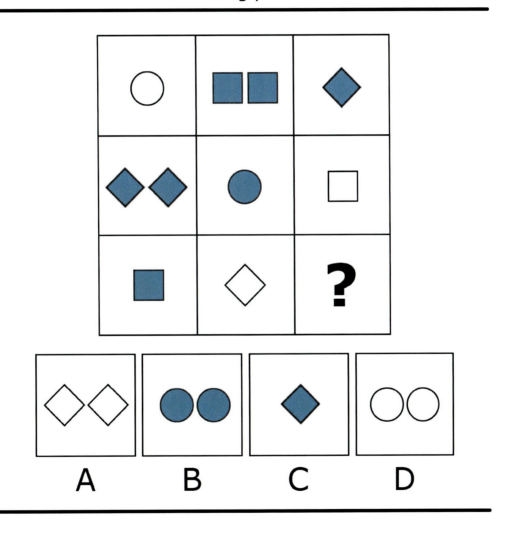

Logical Reasoning Test

Question 7: Which of the following images completes the missing part?

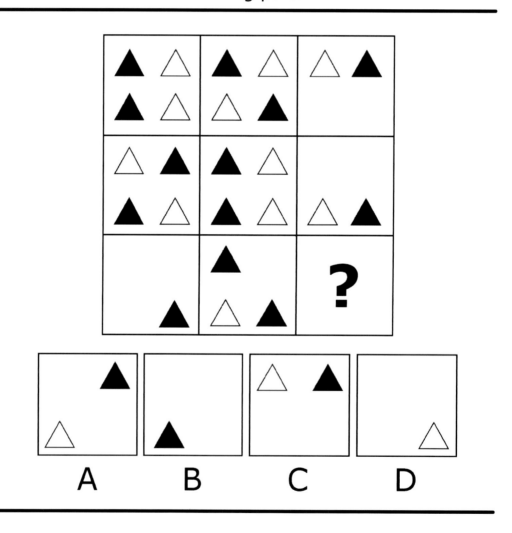

Logical Reasoning Test

Question 8: Which of the following images completes the missing part?

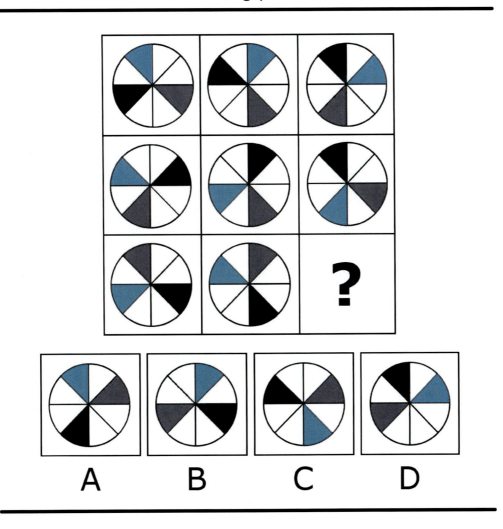

Logical Reasoning Test

Question 9: Which of the following images completes the missing part?

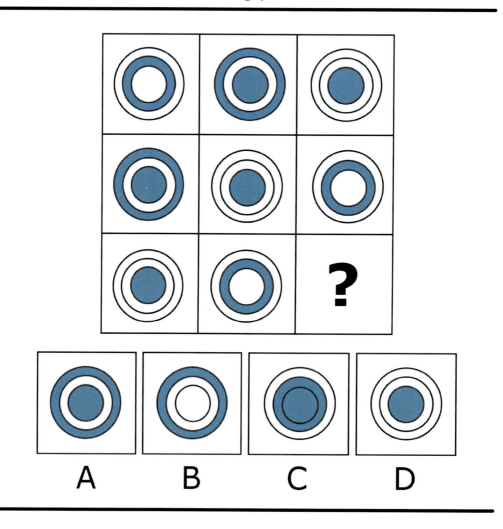

Logical Reasoning Test

Question 10: Which of the following images completes the missing part?

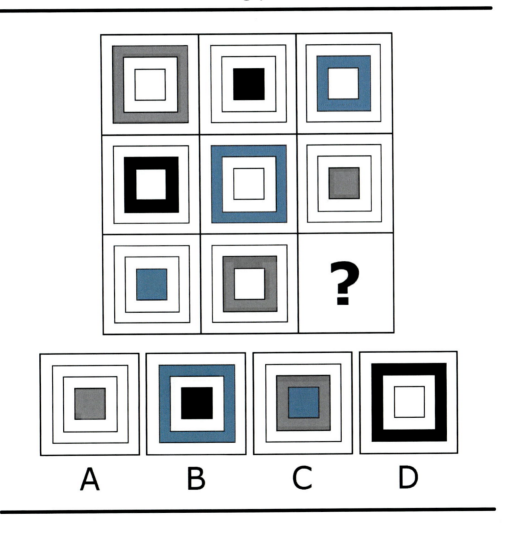

A   B   C   D

Inductive Reasoning Test

Inductive reasoning tests are used to test logical problem-solving ability. They are designed to test your inductive reasoning skills - in other words, to see if you think logically and methodically, which is tested by your ability to recognize patterns in a series. An inductive reasoning test usually involves presenting sentences or series where the goal is to predict the next figure.

Instructions:
Questions present a series of figures with one of the figures replaced by a question mark. Figure out which of the four options is the logical replacement of the question mark.

Inductive Reasoning Test

Question 1:Which figure complete the series?

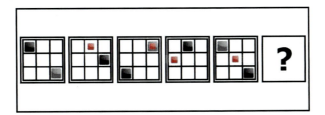

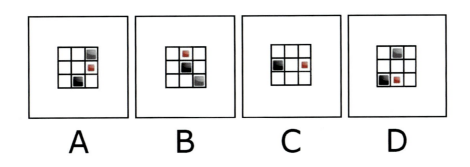

A   B   C   D

Inductive Reasoning Test

Question 2:Which figure complete the series?

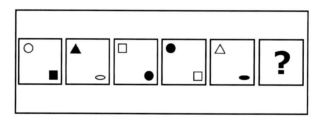

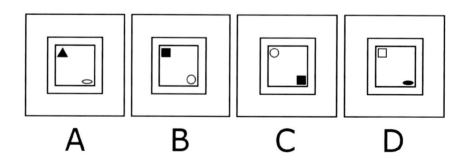

A   B   C   D

Inductive Reasoning Test

Question 3: Which figure complete the series?

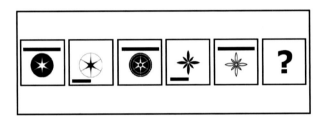

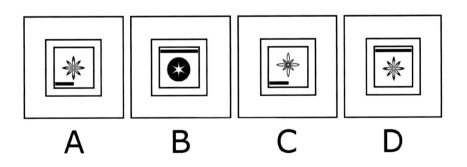

A   B   C   D

Inductive Reasoning Test

Question 4: Which figure complete the series?

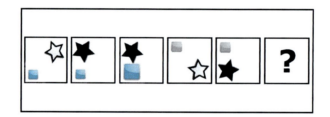

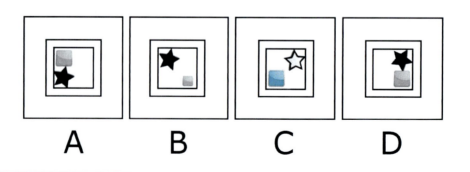

A   B   C   D

Inductive Reasoning Test

Question 5:Which figure complete the series?

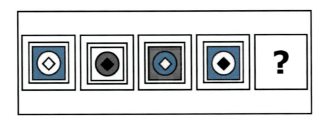

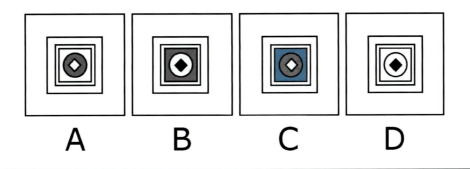

Inductive Reasoning Test

Question 6: Which figure complete the series?

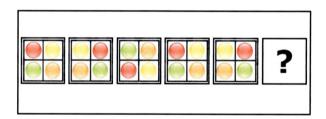

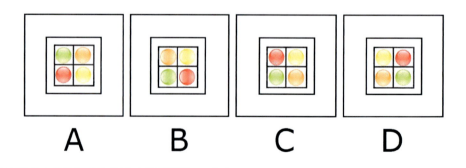

A   B   C   D

Inductive Reasoning Test

Question 7: Which figure complete the series?

A   B   C   D

Inductive Reasoning Test

Question 8: Which figure complete the series?

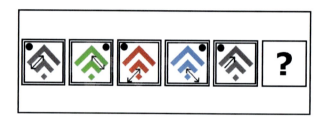

Inductive Reasoning Test

Question 9:Which figure complete the series?

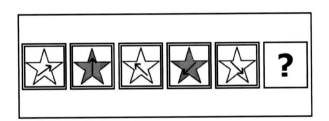

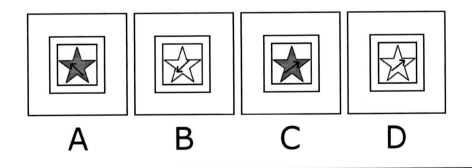

A   B   C   D

Inductive Reasoning Test

Question 10:Which figure complete the series?

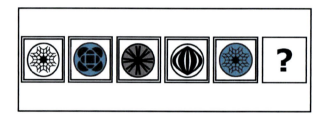

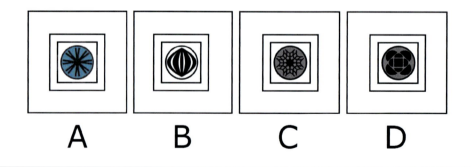

A   B   C   D

Number Series Test

Number series aptitude questions introduce you to mathematical sequences that follow a logical rule and are based on elementary arithmetic. Number series questions are often used in cognitive ability tests. In most cases, they require NOT advanced mathematical knowledge.

Instructions:
All the numbers in the sequence satisfy a certain logical rule, which must be recognized in order to find the missing number. Find the rule that connects the numbers. After you have recognized the rule, you can then derive the missing number.

Number Series Test

Question 1: What number should replace the question mark?

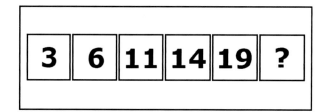

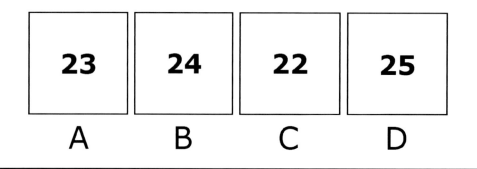

A   B   C   D

Number Series Test

Question 2: What number should replace the question mark?

| 22 | 26 | 32 | 40 | 50 | ? |

54	62	58	60
A	B	C	D

Number Series Test

Question 3: What number should replace the question mark?

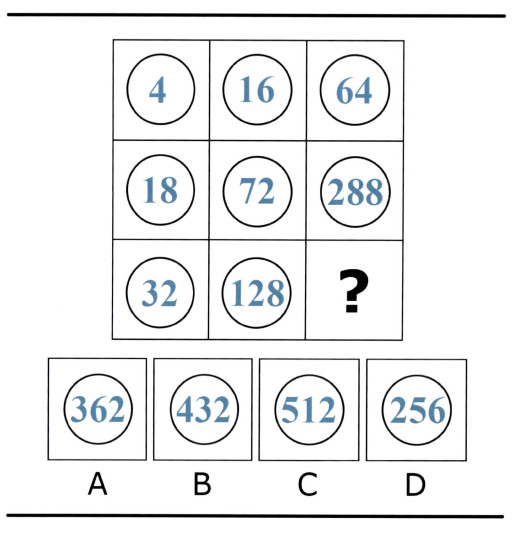

Number Series Test

Question 4: What number should replace the question mark?

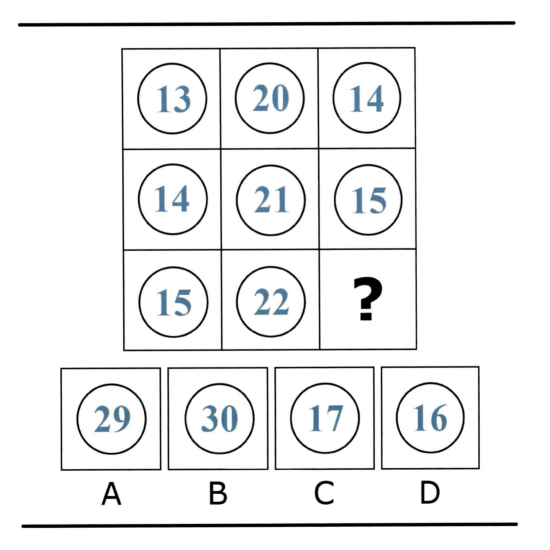

Number Series Test

Question 5: What number should replace the question mark?

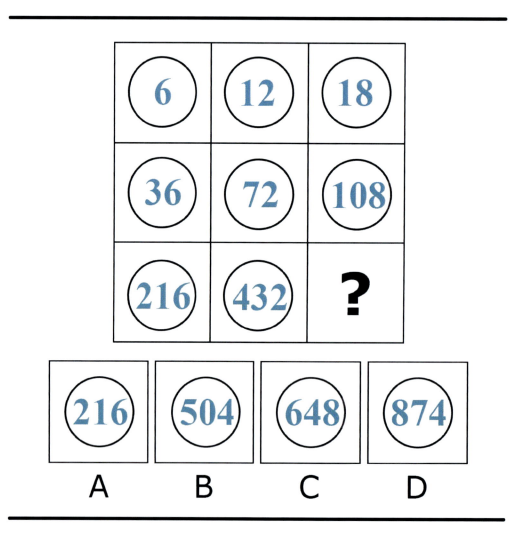

Number Series Test

Question 6: What number should replace the question mark?

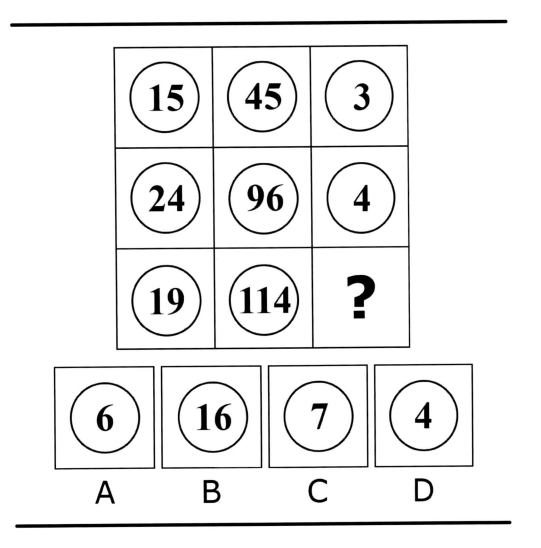

Number Series Test

Question 7: What number should replace the question mark?

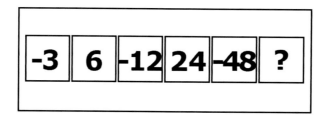

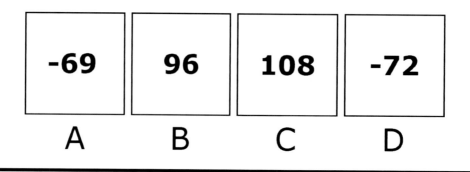

A   B   C   D

Number Series Test

Question 8: What number should replace the question mark?

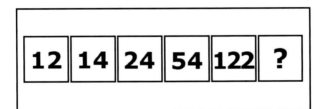

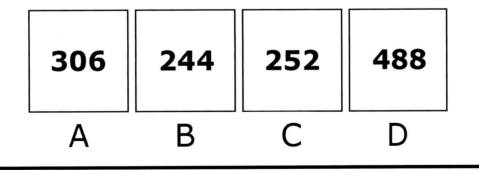

Number Series Test

Question 9: What number should replace the question mark?

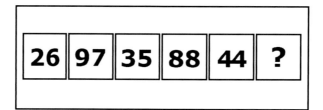

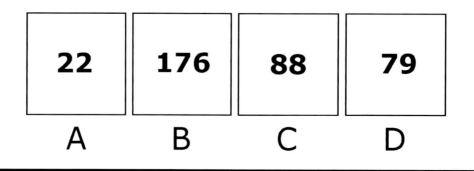

Number Series Test

Question 10: What number should replace the question mark?

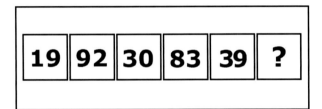

74	80	76	78
A	B	C	D

Verbal Reasoning Test With Analogies

Verbal analogies measure verbal analytic comprehension. This test is about discovering logical relationships between words. Analogy questions test your ability to recognize relationships between pairs of words (and sometimes quantities) or ideas. The questions may involve a number of different word and concept associations, but the question structure remains similar.

Instructions:
These analogies require the use of logic to identify the relationships between words and ideas. Choose the word that correctly completes each analogy.

Verbal Reasoning Test With Analogies

Question 1:Complete the analogy

Pigeon is to bird
as Doberman to ...

Dog	Monkey	Sheep	Mule
A	B	C	D

Verbal Reasoning Test With Analogies

Question 2:Complete the analogy

> Chicken is to worm as man to ...

Cat	Bread	Stone	Wood
A	B	C	D

Verbal Reasoning Test With Analogies

Question 3: Complete the analogy

Paper is to wood
as flour to ...

Wheat	Water	Beer	White
A	B	C	D

Verbal Reasoning Test With Analogies

Question 4:Complete the analogy

Sky is to blue
as soil to ...

Sand	Stone	Black	Fire
A	B	C	D

Verbal Reasoning Test With Analogies

Question 5:Complete the analogy

Doctor is to hospital as lawyer to ...

Restaurant	Airplane	House	Court
A	B	C	D

Verbal Reasoning Test With Analogies

Question 6: Complete the analogy

Father is to son
as uncle to ...

Brother	Nephew	Mother	Sister
A	B	C	D

Verbal Reasoning Test With Analogies

Question 7:Complete the analogy

Painter is to painting
as writer to ...

Pen	Paper	Book	Pencil
A	B	C	D

Verbal Reasoning Test With Analogies

Question 8:Complete the analogy

Astronaut is to space as sailor to ...

Ocean	Ship	River	Boat
A	B	C	D

Verbal Reasoning Test With Analogies

Question 9:Complete the analogy

Shark is to carnivore
as giraffe to ...

Tree	Safari	Forest	Herbivore
A	B	C	D

Verbal Reasoning Test With Analogies

Question 10:Complete the analogy

Happiness is to laughing as sadness to ...

Thinking	Crying	Worrying	Walking
A	B	C	D

ANSWERS

Spatial Reasoning Test
1. D
2. B
3. A
4. D
5. D
6. B
7. D
8. A
9. D
10. C

Diagrammatic Reasoning Test
1. B
2. A
3. B
4. C
5. B
6. C
7. A
8. D
9. A
10. A

Deductive Reasoning Test With Figures
1. B
2. A
3. C
4. C
5. D
6. A
7. B
8. C
9. C
10. C

Inductive Reasoning Figure Series Test
1. C
2. A
3. D
4. B
5. A
6. B
7. D
8. C
9. B
10. A

Math Riddles Test
1. B
2. A
3. D
4. B
5. C
6. D
7. C
8. C
9. B
10. D

Abstract Reasoning Test
1. B
2. D
3. B
4. B
5. C
6. A
7. D
8. B
9. D
10. A

Logical Reasoning Test
1. A
2. D
3. A
4. A
5. D
6. B
7. D
8. A
9. A
10. D

Inductive Reasoning Test
1. C
2. B
3. A
4. A
5. A
6. A
7. B
8. B
9. C
10. D

Number Series Test
1. C
2. B
3. C
4. D
5. C
6. A
7. B
8. C
9. D
10. A

Verbal Reasoning Test With Analogies
1. A
2. B
3. A
4. C
5. D
6. B
7. C
8. A
9. D
10. B

Score Calculation

Less than 19 correct answers: *Please try to focus and practice more*

Between 20-39 correct answers: 90-100

Between 40-59 correct answers: 100-110

Between 60-79 correct answers: 110-120

Between 80-99 correct answers: 120-130

Total 100 correct answers: Your IQ is 130+

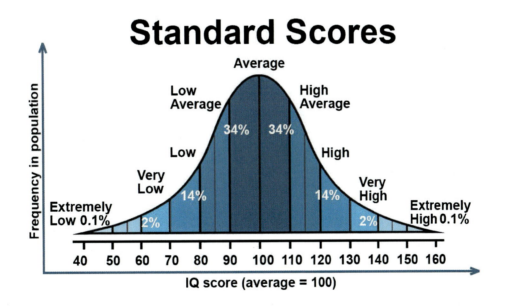

Thank you for your purchase!
I hope you enjoyed this book!

Please consider leaving a review!
https://prfc.nl/go/abreview

Please don't hesitate to contact us if you have any questions!

e-mail: info@perfectconsulting.eu

Made in the USA
Las Vegas, NV
31 March 2024